Pathways, Puzzles, and Possibilities:

A Magical Journey of Transformation

Dear Caroline,

This book reflects a journey
highlighting the resilience of
the human spirit.

Your aunt wanted to share it
to honor your resilience.

Sparkles and sunshine,
Mindy

Pathways, Puzzles, and Possibilities:

A Magical Journey of Transformation

Mindy Schrager

ISBN 13: 978-1-944662-53-0

REALIZATION PRESS

Published by Realization Press, North Carolina, USA.

Cover art Illustration by Mary Louise Smith
Cover Design by Michael Scott
Interior Illustrations by Nicole Jeska

Dedication

I dedicate this book to my mother, Miriam, whose own journey influenced mine in both positive and negative ways. To my father, Julius, who modeled integrity, caring, and an understanding of value. To my husband, Jim, who may not always understand my journeys but continues to love me along the way.

I also dedicate this book to all those individuals in my life who could see beneath the surface to the truth of who I am.

I further dedicate this book to all those who have been bullied in some way for who or what you are. May you have the courage to know the beautiful truth that lies beneath the surface.

Table of Contents

About the Book

Our life journeys cross many landscapes, some where the terrain is green and lush and others where it is rocky or mountainous. I invite you to go on a series of magical explorations where lessons are learned, pathways are forged, and obstacles are overcome. While the characters include gnomes, dragons, and even a fairy princess, this is built on a true story that highlights the importance of being kind to yourself, aligning your inner resources, and designing your own unique life tapestry—allowing the world to see the truth of who you are.

As we each take responsibility for our pathways in life and the possibilities we create, how do we solve the various life puzzles presented to us? Consider:

- How do you feel you fit in and belong with your family?
- Are you looking for your "tribe," or have you already found that connection?
- Are you surrounded by naysayers or cheerleaders?
- Do you see obstacles or opportunities?
- Do you honor yourself or allow yourself to be bullied or bully yourself?
- Do you allow the truth of who you are to shine through?

BONUS

Each chapter of the book ties to a specific transformational concept. Take a brief "quiz" associated with each concept to gain a better understanding of where you are on your own transformational journey. Check out the chapter summary that most resonates for you and take that quiz or look at all five. Each has a transformational process you can use to create new pathways and possibilities. To access this information go to: *https://systemsofchange.com/bonus/*

Chapter One
Introduction to the
Metaphorical Journey

Many years ago in a land called Jersey in a village called The Lawn, a little girl was born and they named her Mindy. She was told she was unexpected, an accident, while at the same time she heard how her dad had always wanted a girl.

There were the usual trials and tribulations of growing up. Running around the house and falling forehead first into the corner of a wall, being bitten in the face by a dog she innocently bent down to pet, and getting a concussion after some creative but not well-thought-out fun time. There were also the good times of growing up—friends, family, exploring the village, taking dancing, singing, and musical instrument lessons, and sometimes trips to the kingdom they called Big York.

Then when Mindy was five, the family moved to another village called The Woodlake. Shortly thereafter, Mindy's mom started a teaching job, part-time at first and then full-time. Being the only latchkey kid in the neighborhood was a bit of a challenge although kind neighbors kept an eye out for her.

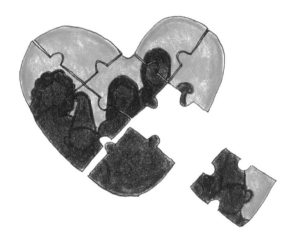

Mindy made some friends in the neighborhood and shared her deepest secret with her "best friend." She wet her bed. Every morning she would wake up, hating how she felt and then hearing the words of her mother's frustration. Various doctors and other treatments were tried, but, despite her best efforts and prayers and pleas for it to stop, nothing seemed to work.

Then it was decided she needed to incorporate more fun things into her world. Off to summer camp she went. At first it was day camp, but then for various adult reasons it was decided an overnight camp would be better. Her secret was shared in whispers to counselors who kept it mostly quiet at first.

However, in Mindy's thirteenth year, the secret was announced in the school cafeteria by her "best friend," and the camp counselors could no longer keep it quiet. Already feeling betrayed by her body, the events that happened with the children took away her sense of safety. Mindy's anger at herself and others grew, but she had to bury it deep inside in order to survive.

In her 16th year, the bedwetting suddenly stopped, but the damage had already been done. When she reached her 18th year, Mindy escaped to another land, this one called Pennson, where she started college and left her earlier life behind. Her first year was full of adjustments, and she began to find her way and new friends. She opted to study the language of foreign lands, having chosen this particular school because it offered Italian along with French, German, and many others.

In her junior year, she chose to visit one of those foreign lands, France. She had magnificent adventures and also picked up a bad habit or two, namely smoking and drinking. She returned home, finished college, and then moved to another land called Massach to attend graduate school. Mindy had the good fortune to visit and study in another foreign land, Switzerland, as part of her graduate school studies.

All the while deep inside, a variety of physical manifestations were being created, built on what she had buried deep. These physical manifestations led her to embark on a journey of healing and learning which has spanned many decades. Many layers buried in emotions, trauma, family lineage, and the like were uncovered and excavated during this time.

During the healing journey, Mindy had the opportunity to write a metaphorical hero's journey as an assignment in an NLP class. The heroes born out of that first story, Humphrey and LouLou Belle, are the first ones introduced in this book. After attending an improv workshop and having a meltdown, the facilitator suggested several one-on-one improv appointments. During those sessions, Mindy uncovered a love of writing, and more characters appeared through the healing stories she wrote.

Having always loved the story of Humphrey and the resonance with his being born into a family where he didn't feel he belonged, Mindy toyed with the idea of publishing the story. While doubts abounded, the need to share the story of the impact of bullying and the journey to find one's true self shone through.

As the final chapter was written, Mindy looked back and realized that, while the story unfolded over years, it somehow all weaved together—like a magical tapestry or life mosaic with the pieces all falling into place.

We hope you enjoy this metaphorical journey of self-discovery, following pathways, uncovering possibilities, overcoming obstacles, seeing new perspectives, and building a cohesive inner team. All in the support of nurturing a dream and finding the way back to one's true self.

Sparkles and sunshine,
Mindy and her metaphorical inner team

Chapter Two

Humphrey and LouLou Belle

One day Humphrey told me a story about how he had helped one of the maids of the forest journey to the Land of Possibilities and there find the keys to her future. I asked him if was willing to share how he had gotten to be so wise about knowing what to do for others.

This is Humphrey's story, a magical tale of self-discovery.

As a young gnome, Humphrey learned the secret of traveling to the Land of Possibilities. He was born into a family of elves who weren't quite expecting a gnome to join their ranks. Humphrey learned early on what it felt like to be different and not quite fit in or belong. Whenever he got sad and lonely, he would journey to another vista where life looked very different—like a kaleidoscope of ever-changing patterns, colors, and possibilities. Of course, being who he was, Humphrey did work to fit in by dressing in elves' clothing like the rest of the family, but his discontent grew steadily over the years. And so, as a young man, Humphrey set out to find his way, take control of his life, and seek out his calling, his life's purpose.

But as a gnome in elves' clothing, what was Humphrey to do? Well, he traveled the globe, met many wonderful people, and experimented with different types of métiers. After a number of years, he recognized that he had a gift for helping others and getting them to work in community with each other. However, he also realized that while he had journeyed very far from home to find his calling, he missed his woods and his family and friends. Humphrey decided to return back home to the forest where he was born. He took with him some of the special gifts he had acquired over the years including his magical snow globe, his brass kaleidoscope, and his miniature merry-go-round. All of these small treasures reminded him of the people and resources he had found through his journey.

As he arrived back home, he could hear the cheers in the forest. The town folk were truly happy to see Humphrey again because without him everything felt more chaotic and a bit less colorful. And after all his travels, Humphrey was really ready to be back home, but this time it was on his own terms. He built a log cabin on the edge of the forest surrounded by his family and friends. When he looked out, he saw the beauty of his future laid out like a vast green meadow dotted with colorful wildflowers. He was content, but he needed a job.

He again traveled to the Land of Possibilities to discover the keys to unlocking his career fulfillment. Lo and behold, he found an opportunity at the king's court where he was promptly hired as a jester. Little did he know that day he would have an experience that would change the course of his life forever.

A dragon had made its way into the palace and blocked Humphrey from moving forward. Humphrey could hear his little inner gnome whispering in his ear, "Run the other way; that's a really big dragon; you can't do this. What are you—nuts?" But having learned from experience that he was the master of his own destiny and knowing he had a few tricks up his sleeve, Humphrey sucked it up, walked into the void, faced his fears, and was able to find the key to all of his internal resources. Brave Humphrey was able to subdue the dragon and turn him into a wonderful guardian and protector for the palace.

As a reward the king bestowed on Humphrey all the rights of a person of his honorable stature along with some magical keys. Humphrey also got a key to his own personal gym, which was a good thing because after subduing that dragon he realized he was really out of shape. But the best thing of all was that a star was named after Humphrey, whose light thereafter shone brightly both day and night.

As a leader in his own way, Humphrey created a wonderful community within the court, which felt totally aligned with his purpose. He felt fulfillment every day as he walked from his home through the meadow of his future and into the king's court. He also dabbled in the healing arts with his friends in the forest, knowing that was one of his keys.

Humphrey was held in high esteem at the court until they forced him to retire at the age of 67. But being true to his calling, Humphrey didn't fully retire. Instead he turned to the healing arts full-time, and he even added storytelling to his bag of skills.

And that's how I was able to hear the story of the maid who lived in the forest. But then that's Humphrey's story to tell.

෨   ෬

My name is Humphrey and I'm here to tell you a fairy tale.

Once upon a time on the outskirts of the forest, there lived a fair maid. Her name was LouLou Belle.

LouLou Belle spent her days foraging for treasures.

She looked in caves, on treetops, in river beds, and under toadstools. Actually, I met her when she knocked over my toadstool. None too happy was I. She always tried really hard to find things she thought villagers in the neighboring town would like.

"I just want them to like me and welcome me into their homes," she told me once.

One day I saw her sitting by the side of the road looking sad and dejected. Uh-oh, I thought, and, sure enough, some grand poobah had laughed her out of his office. Not only that but he threw all her treasures on the floor. She salvaged what she could, but he broke some of her favorite items (big meanie).

So I gave her my hankie, told her to dry her eyes, and got her to follow me back to our forest. That day I shared with her my treasures and a message that would change the rest of her life (for the better, of course; this is a fairy tale).

My jester hat. And I reminded her it's always important to keep 'em happy, live with joy in your heart, and never let them see you sweat.

My snow globe. I told her it was magical and could take her anywhere she wanted to go.

"But how?" she asked.

And my simple reply: "The key is within you."

That statement seemed to irritate her, and I sent her on her way to ponder. So what was the first thing she did? She asked the creatures of the forest for the key. They all kept telling her what I had said: "The key is within."

Perplexed and tired, she went back to her hut. She pulled up a shade and looked up at the moonlit sky and simply asked, "Show me the key."

And that night as she dreamt, four keys fell from the sky:

- the key of wisdom
- the key of power
- the key of compassion
- the key of strength

But they were big heavy keys and they wouldn't work with the snow globe. The journey to find the key continued, and, with each of the passing days, she again asked, "What is the key that is within me?"

And more keys kept appearing:

- She saw the image of her star shining outward.

- She realized the choices in life were hers alone to make.

- She learned it was time to commit to loving herself on all levels.

- She understood she needed to find contentment with all the pieces she had and, for those she didn't have, to believe in the Land of Possibilities.

- And in the end it truly was not how she imagined herself reflected by others but what she knew deep inside she was, she wanted, and was possible.

And that's when she saw the image of a snow globe from long, long ago, a snow globe with a wooden panel that pulled apart to reveal a secret compartment that held a key within.

She ran to my house, got the snow globe, and, with all her keys, entered the Land of Possibilities. She had remembered to bring some of her best treasures, and she traded them for Possibilities (in this case cash) and returned home.

She bought a little house in the center of town and set it up so she could display and sell her treasures to the many people who now stopped by. One day as LouLou Belle was thinking about how much life had changed since she had found the Land of Possibilities and built from what was deep inside, she found a special treasure.

It was a wooden plaque that said: "Whether you know it or not, you are already there—you are the beauty…the power…the wisdom…the passion…the knowledge…the fire…the calm…the heart & soul…you are the star of your being."

I looked at her in wonder as she said this because I knew all along that LouLou Bell meant "dear beauty." And that she is. While much of the story is yet to reveal, all I can say at this point is, "Go for it, LouLou Belle. Let your star shine bright and don't let 'em see you sweat."

Chapter Three
On the Other Side of the Rainbow

In a kingdom on the colorless side of the rainbow, there lived a kind witch by the name of Glenda. Glenda always had a smile on her face as she spent her days helping those in the kingdom. Over her lifetime, Glenda had developed strong skills as a kind witch but had become restless of late. She had grown tired of wearing that same white, poofy, kind witch outfit every day. Everything in her life was white— colorful yet colorless at the same time.

She was 75, and, while she looked darned good for her age, she knew she was approaching the top of the age range for kind witches. She also recognized that once her next birthday approached, the magic of her good looks would start to fade. Her friend Humphrey, the gnome, said she was entering a midlife crisis.

Dear Humphrey. He was actually part of the problem. While Glenda had lived in a world that was colorless,

Humphrey had started introducing her to color. After he retired as the court jester in the kingdom on the other side of the rainbow, he shed his elves' clothing, owned his inner gnome, and bought a second home on the colorless side of the rainbow (Glenda's side).

He brought his magical ways and his prized possessions with him. He had shown Glenda his kaleidoscope and how it broke up the colors of the rainbow. He also gave her some beautiful colored stones and scarves from his travels around the world that she had carefully placed throughout the comfy carriage house she lived in. She wondered why he didn't share the colors with more people in the kingdom, but he always said it wasn't his place. His message to her was to find the emerald of her heart.

Glenda had also started to question her chosen path. She had accepted the magic wand of kind witches from her mother. When she had tried to pass that wand to Esmerelda, her daughter had refused to take it. Esmerelda had instead decided that she wanted to explore the land on the other side of the rainbow. She said she wanted to discover things for herself, not just do what her parents said without questioning.

Glenda sighed as she sat back on her comfy couch looking out at the colorless light of the kingdom. She knew that to get to the other side she had to pay the rainbow toll collector. The price was a bag of gold. She had saved a long time so that Esmerelda could go, and she knew it would take a while longer for her to obtain the necessary coins. She also was afraid of letting the members of the kingdom (including the king who had paid for her carriage house) see her travel. She didn't want them to think she didn't wish to be with them anymore. She started wondering if it might be best to go at night when it was less likely she would be seen.

Just as she let out a sigh, Humphrey rang the doorbell. He could tell she was deep in thought and asked her why she looked so far away. She shared her desire to visit the other side of the rainbow and her concerns about the time and money to get there. He told her if she really wanted to go and go now, he could use his magical snow globe to transport her to the other side. However, once there, she would have to find her way.

She knew she had to do something. She made a deal with Humphrey to meet the following evening and then made a list of tasks to complete. The next morning, she left a message with the king letting him know she was going to take some of her accumulated vacation time. She was nervous as she told him but knew deep in her heart that she had to go. She packed a few things including stones of various colors—gold for wisdom, red for power, emerald green for heart, and the turquoise of communication. When Humphrey stopped by, he let her know that her magic wand would actually get her there.

While frustrated he hadn't told her that the prior evening, she thanked Humphrey for letting her know, waved her magic wand, and off she went to the land on the other side of the rainbow. When she arrived, she felt very uncertain and full of doubts. Everything seemed so different. However, as she looked around, she found there was actually a clear path that wound its way throughout the land. Putting one foot in front of another, step by step, she moved forward and began to understand the lay of the land.

While she felt more confident and continued moving forward on the path, she also realized she was feeling alone. As she progressed further, she felt the presence of some of the fairies and devas that lived in the colorless kingdom she had travelled from. These thoughtful fairies and devas had wanted to make sure she was safe and protected on her journey, so they tagged along. She thanked them and continued following the path.

She entered the gold village of wisdom. In the center of village was a wise man. He called her over.

"What is a kind witch doing on the other side of the rainbow?"

"I am looking to find the emerald of my heart."

"In order to pass out of the village of wisdom, you must answer an important question." With that the wise man asked, "Why are you looking for the emerald of your heart here?"

Glenda thoughtfully responded, "Because on the colorless side, I can only live in my heart through my head."

The wise man smiled and told her she could pass. The fairies and devas were clapping as she continued to move along the path.

Looking up, she could see some of the archangels smiling upon her. The ones that revealed themselves predominantly were Michael, Metatron, and Gabriel. She smiled back at them and asked them what they wanted her to know.

18

This journey was like a monopoly game with obstacles and prizes, so she thought they might help her move forward on the path.

Michael told her to think with her heart about what she was destined to do. Metatron suggested she look for that which was most difficult to see within herself. Gabriel suggested she gaze up at the stars and draw them into her so that the light shone from within her.

And so she moved forward. She took a moment to rest and spoke with her heart. Your life is to be of service. You can honor this calling until age 150 as a fairy princess. You can still serve the masses but only those who want help. Glenda then thought about what within might stop her from this path. As she considered, she stepped forward. Unbeknownst to her, she had entered the red village of power, which was ruled by a fearsome dragon.

Before she saw the dragon, she heard him. "Who goes there?" he said.

"I am a visitor from the colorless side of the rainbow, looking to find the emerald of my heart."

"First you must pass by me," said the dragon. "Tell me what you fear most in your quest. If you lie, I will know and then you will have to face a test."

Glenda wondered how best to answer this. She knew she was drawn to find the emerald of the heart, but many in her life had been skeptical.

"I am afraid that this quest is for naught," said Glenda.

"False," responded the dragon. "Having answered incorrectly, you must now pass another test."

What could the dragon's test be, she wondered in fear. Could she pass it? Was it worth the effort? Should she just go back? No, I am surrounded by fairies, devas, and archangels who believe in me, she said to herself. I will go forward.

As the fearsome dragon faced her, she thought of all those who had doubted her in her life.

Then she heard the dragon say, "You must walk through fire for me to allow you out of this village."

And with that the dragon created a wall of fire in front of Glenda. Glenda took a deep breath, looked up at the stars in the sky, and reached up in her mind's eye to draw one inside as Gabriel had suggested. As she did so, her soul and incarnational stars grew brighter, and she knew in her head, her heart, and her gut that there was no turning back.

Cautiously she moved through the bright wall of fire. As she did, she felt the star within her burn brightly; she felt the layers of sadness and disappointment melt from her body along with her poofy white gown. As she came out the other side, her daughter, who was living on the other side of the rainbow, was there to hug her and wrapped her with a beautiful multicolored gown. The dragon then again asked her what she feared most.

"I fear that once I find the emerald of my heart I will not belong anywhere—with anyone—and that would destroy me."

With that, the dragon turned his scales to emerald green, reflecting what he saw in Glenda's heart. As Glenda hugged her daughter, she realized that Esmeralda had gotten it right. Her daughter worked with the dragon helping people from both sides of the rainbow find the emerald of their hearts. How appropriate for a girl named Esmeralda, the Spanish word for Emerald.

With the stars shining bright within her, the emerald of her heart exposed, and surrounded by fairies, devas, archangels, and her daughter, Glenda smiled. She could see the turquoise village of communication just ahead of her.

As she arrived in the village center, she saw a gnome seated there. The gnome let Glenda know that she must answer a question or return immediately to the colorless side of the rainbow, forgetting all that she learned and never to return. If she got it correct, he would tell her the path of light to return anytime.

"What will you do with the emerald of your heart?" he asked.

"I want to share it with the people on the colorless side of the rainbow. I want to bring the color out into the light," she said.

The gnome let Glenda know that she had earned the right to learn the alternate route back to the colorless side of the rainbow, the way without a toll. He showed her the start of the bridge that crossed the base of the rainbow. Before she set off, he placed in her hand a lovely velvet pouch that was filled with hundreds of small but beautiful and sparkly emeralds.

As Glenda continued on the path to the bridge, she moved forward step by step with the knowledge and the power she had acquired, and feeling the backing of the people, fairies, devas, and archangels who supported her—everything she needed to bring color to the colorless side of the rainbow. The color she would share to support transformation and growth for those who wanted to change. She was inspired to start her new role as a fairy princess, being of service for the next 75 years.

Glenda got closer and closer to the edge of the bridge in the colorless land. At the end of the bridge, Humphrey met her in his green hat, a hat he'd worn in her honor. The gnome in that last village was his cousin from the non-elf side of his family, so he knew what had taken place and was there to meet her. He walked with her as she put one foot in front of another as her path continued to appear clearly in front of her.

Many in the town were surprised to see the colors she could now use as a fairy princess. She had purchased even more stones and scarves and colorful trinkets when Humphrey took her to LouLou Belle's shop on their way back home.

While many could see the colors she shared, there were others who couldn't perceive them at all. As she approached the castle, she took out the velvet pouch and tossed handfuls of emeralds into the air and onto the ground in front of her. As she did so, the castle and the area surrounding it reflected the beautiful emerald green, feeling lush and expansive.

The king saw Glenda approach and came out to welcome her back from vacation. He could see that she was different and that some in his kingdom liked the change. He invited her to tell her tale, which she did gladly. As she spoke, she firmly stated her desire to become known as Glenda the Fairy Princess who worked with only those who wished to change and see the colors. Since he was a wise king, he could see the possibilities this offered in his kingdom.

Now when Glenda sits on her comfy couch and looks out on the castle, she sees a city that reflects the emerald of her heart. She feels surrounded by the love and support of the fairies, devas, and angels, her friends, family, and those who can see the color. And for those who can't yet perceive the colors, Glenda now has the wisdom, the power, and the compassion to see their magic too.

Chapter Four
The Story of the Contrarians

In a village not too far away from Humphrey, LouLou Belle and Glenda, there lived a wise but egotistical king. He decided that he would do whatever he could to leave a legacy more memorable than anyone who had lived before or after him. In his wisdom, he decided to make the kingdom a most enjoyable land.

As part of this, he established Gameland with fun activities of different kinds. One of these was a living chess game that played out in the center of the village every day. The villagers portrayed the different chess pieces, and the objective was to find the townsperson who was most capable of protecting the king.

One of the village girls, Sophie, decided that she would learn to play this chess game to the very best of her ability. It was a way to escape her daily life with her parents and a job as a housekeeper that was only okay. Her father brought fear into her life, always questioning, asking *what if*, and believing that everything would go away in the end. Her mother brought self-doubt and judgment into her life, always asking why she couldn't be more like the daughters of every other villager in the town. More helpful, more courageous, more intelligent. More, more, more.

When Sophie heard about the chess game, she decided that she would find a way to master every move of every piece. While most villagers were content to play the same piece game after game, Sophie learned them all. When she was acting as the knight, she believed she understood what the pawn might do. When she portrayed the queen, she thought she knew how to be most protective of her king. Sophie was always surprised because no one ever played their piece exactly the same way. Finally, after years of trying the approach of being everyone but no one at the same time, Sophie decided now was the chance to find out who she really was. It was Sophie's first "choice."

She soon set out on a journey through the surrounding villages. First, she went to the woods close to the castle, and there she found the retired jester's house. She realized he was a gnome dressed as an elf and thought he must not be very comfortable within himself. However, when Humphrey shared his story with her, she realized that he, just like she, had gone on a journey of self-discovery. And she recognized that all those "other people" her mother would have preferred that she would be were not who she wanted to be.

Next, she went to the village on the colorless of the rainbow. There she heard the legend of Glenda, the kind witch who had become a fairy princess. She came to understand that while she had been trying to be everyone other than herself, she had missed out on the many beautiful things and people whom she had met in her life. She had been too busy trying to be colorless like everyone else and had failed to see all the ways color supported her life.

As she continued her travels, she came upon a village called The Land of the Contrarians. Sounds like my life, she mused, and she decided to check it out. Everyone she talked to was an expert counter-exampler, always finding a reason why something wasn't possible. When she pointed out an inaccuracy in their counter example, they got nervous and scared. She also realized that they were constantly talking about why they couldn't do something. When she asked what would happen if they could do something, they became flustered and started to hyperventilate. She found interesting behavior patterns among the contrarians, who were filled with conflict, walked in zigzag patterns a lot, and never quite committed to anything for fear they might miss out on something else.

And as she got to the center of town, she saw a stone tablet with a series of questions for all visitors to review. It was the Contrarian Test and the questions were:

1. Are you always trying to be someone other than yourself?

2. Do you feel like opportunity is for others and not for you?

3. Do you always find counter-examples?

4. When you get close to what you think you want, do you become afraid?

Sophie made her choices in responding to the test, and, when she got to the end, she heard a booming voice say, "You are a Contrarian too. You should stay in this village forever so that you may be with others of your kind."

Sophie pondered and pondered, not knowing what to do next. She knew she didn't want to be a Contrarian, but she didn't know who else to be. She decided to keep walking. Deeper and deeper into the woods she went, and the next thing she knew she was at the edge of a cliff with deep, deep water at the base. She realized that the only way to the next village was through this water. But it looked so deep, so terrifying, and she wasn't sure what to do.

She decided to sit down in the forest and think about what made her a Contrarian.

- If I let myself be seen, I'm afraid that I will be mocked for who I am, *but,* if I don't let myself be seen, I'm afraid I will never be happy.

- If I let myself be heard, I'm afraid that my words will be ridiculed, and people will think me stupid, *but,* if I don't let myself be heard, I will be trapped in a prison of my own making.

- If I get close to someone, I'm afraid they will see me for an imposter and leave, *but,* if I allow someone to go away, I am afraid that I will be forever alone.

- If I believe in myself, I know no one else will, *but,* if I don't believe in myself, maybe someone will try to help.

- If I hope, I will only be disappointed, *but,* if I don't hope, there is nothing to live for.

And with that she started to cry. Hearing the sounds of her cries, the animals in the forest started telling her to jump into the water and make her way out of the Land of the Contrarians.

"But I'm afraid," she said, "and don't know how to find my way. How can I speak up when I never have been heard before? How can I let myself be seen for who I am when I don't really know who I am? How do I let myself hope when I've always been disappointed in the past?"

The animals started to chuckle.

"Why are you laughing at me?" she yelled. "Stop it!"

"We are not laughing at you," they said. "We just know that you know something that you don't think you know. It is like a riddle and that made us chuckle."

"And what is it that you know I know that I don't know I know?" she asked in frustration?

"You have the key; you have always had the key. It is hidden deep in your heart, and, if you dive into the water, you will hear it in the stillness. Besides what is the worst that happens if you jump?"

"I'll die," she said.

And the animals responded, "Aren't you dying a little bit at a time already?"

And with that Sophie made a choice—Sophie's second "choice." She dove into that murky water in search of the key within her heart. The emerald within her heart, the love and the knowledge that she knew deep within revealed what she was meant to be and do. And somehow, someway, she would always find the way and what she needed as long as she held onto the key within her heart.

As Sophie walked away from her past, she realized that making a difference in the lives of others was the strong and immutable force in her life helping her to remember that we are all part of *All That Is*.

Chapter Five
Journey to the Mill House

As Sophie climbed out of the water on the opposite bank, she held tight to the thought of the key within her heart. She was tired and wet but exhilarated at the same time. Not too far from where she came out of the water, Sophie saw a glen in the woods. As she got closer, she could see that there was a small stream and a bridge that crossed over it. The sun was shining brightly, reflecting on the water. The bridge looked like a most inviting place to rest.

She lay down on the bridge feeling the warm noontime sun on her face and started to doze. Just as she was about to fall asleep, she was awakened by a voice.

"Do you want to go explore?"

Sophie opened her eyes and looked up into the face of a gnome. Scared at first, she took a deep breath and asked, "Explore what?"

"Explore the future and discover the path you need to walk to get from here to there."

"Oh, okay," stammered Sophie.

As she stood up to follow the gnome across the bridge, she thought she should find out with whom she was speaking and asked the gnome for his name. After all, she had been told never to speak with strangers, and she always felt compelled to do as she was told.

"I am a gnome from the other side of the rainbow, and a wise gnome am I."

Still uncertain, Sophie decided there was no harm as the gnome was pretty small.

When they came to the end of the bridge, Sophie could see they were headed into the woods. She was glad to find that there was a pretty stone path because the woods looked a little scary to her. As they walked following the path, the gnome asked Sophie what scared her most about the future. Sophie thought for a moment, and the first thing that came to mind was *what if*. And with that, the hail started to fall, and Sophie felt each hailstone as it struck any and all unprotected spots on her body. It was similar to the pain she felt when she thought of *what if I can't do what I want, what if no one likes me, what if I can't make a living, what if, what if, what if.* And with that last *what if*, the hail stopped, and they came upon a big, beautiful old tree.

Wow, look at that tree. And at that big hole in the trunk. It appears large enough for me to sit down in, she mused. Being tired from her thoughts and uncomfortable from being pelted by those hailstones, Sophie let out a deep sigh as she sat down.

The gnome came up beside her and asked, "Have you always been afraid of *what if*?"

Sophie nodded. "My father was always worried about what if everything goes away, and my mother always asked what if you could only be like those other villagers' daughters."

"And how many of your *what if* scenarios have come to pass?"

"A few have from time to time," Sophie commented, "but most of the time I worried for naught."

"So what is most important to you about this future you are heading towards," queried the gnome?"

"Making a difference for others, being loved, and having a comfortable lifestyle," she said with a sigh.

"So what if, instead of asking what if I can't, you were to look at the ways in which you could. In other words, look at the steps you need to take, rather than the obstacles you might encounter. Just think for a minute about how you would get to that future you want. Do you really think that would make a difference? What if it did?" the gnome said as he smiled.

And just at that moment, the sun broke through the clouds, and Sophie could see the moisture glistening on the trees and the plants.

"I guess I could try," she said to the gnome as she stood up.

The two of them continued on the path, and the gnome asked, "Is there anything else from your past that keeps you from getting where you want to go?"

"Well, I have always been somewhat of a contrarian, doing what people told me I could not and not succeeding where people thought I would. It feels like no one really believes in me, and that makes everything more difficult. I guess I should move past that, but it makes me mad sometimes."

"Did you ever wonder what made them be like that?"

"Not really. I just set out to prove them wrong."

The gnome could see that Sophie was getting angry just thinking about it and was about to say something when the skies opened up and a torrential rain began to fall. Sophie ran for cover with the gnome close at her heels. She had spotted a small tree house not too far away.

As they came in from the rain, the gnome continued the conversation by asking, "What if they were doing it to keep you from getting hurt?

"If that were the case, why would they be so hurtful?"

"Maybe they thought they were helping you, or maybe they didn't know what you really needed."

"So you mean they didn't do it intentionally?" Sophie said with a perplexed look on her face.

"No, maybe not, and by staying angry with them, you are actually hurting yourself."

"I never thought about it that way," Sophie said. And with that she stood up, flung wide the door to the tree house, and decided it was time to continue towards her future.

While it was still raining, Sophie knew she needed to continue on the path in order to get out of the woods by nightfall. She didn't know that at this time of day a huge flock of birds flew from a cave right past the tree house. So just as she stepped outside, they swarmed past her. A few actually flew into her and with the strength of their flight knocked her to the ground. Face down she fell on the soft moss-covered ground. The shock of the surprise "attack" and the strength with which she fell knocked the wind out of her and she started to cry. The gnome came scurrying over. (Given his height, birds didn't usually fly into him.)

He helped Sophie to sit up and told her that those birds always flew through the woods at that time.

"If only I had known the rules of the woods, I wouldn't have gotten hurt."

"Are you hurt," asked the gnome, "or feeling rather foolish?"

Sophie didn't answer but she thought long and hard about what he had asked. She realized she had gotten scared because she felt like the birds were coming after her. And it had happened just after she got angry. It seemed like every time she stood up for herself or thought to do something different, something or someone came after her, telling her why she should, couldn't, or shouldn't. Would she ever be able to feel like she could just follow her own rules instead of being what others thought she should be or do or think?

She sighed again, then stood up, and dusted herself off, and they continued towards the other side of the woods. She realized she had been sighing a lot. Sometimes it felt like life was just overwhelming, and she didn't know where to begin. Sometimes it felt like no matter how hard she tried she kept repeating the same patterns day after day, month after month, year after year.

Why can't I get out of my own way? Why do I do things that aren't good for me even knowing that they may hurt me? Why do I keep myself from being successful?

These questions were still running through her head as they came out of the woods. Sophie thought the area looked familiar. In fact, she had come full circle and was back in the same glen. But it looked different somehow. She started to walk towards the bridge but then changed her mind since she didn't want to cross the same bridge again.

A splash of color caught her eye and she saw a beautiful lotus flower in the still, dark waters nearby. She had heard that the lotus inspires a person, that whenever faced with trouble, no matter how dark the waters may get, he or she will rise above and let the beautiful flower in them bloom as long as they have a pure and sincere heart.

She thought of that lotus as she started walking, looking for an area of the stream that ran deeper. The gnome walked alongside her. They both wondered why the water was so shallow. Up ahead Sophie spotted a mill house that was built to cross the water. She wondered if there were a key in that house to make the water run more swiftly and more deeply.

As she approached, she realized that this was the magic mill house that she heard about as a girl. Drawing on her memory, she thought of the three pieces to the puzzle and wondered if she could remember the clues.

First, she went to the front door and lifted the special lever. As she did so, she thought, *I am who I am and that is okay.* She then saw how lifting that special lever opened a space under the threshold. This then allowed her to push apart the two false panels in the front. With that the thought came into her head that *I can do what I want to do and make a difference in the lives of others.* Then she rushed over to the wheel on the side of the house. As she turned it, she noticed that the water downstream started to flow more freely. And she realized that what she needed would come to her even if she had to work hard to keep the flow going. After all, even if the tide of the stream did ebb and flow, she could always follow it downstream to the ocean. She had a found a wellspring—a source of continual supply.

The gnome came rushing over to tell her she needed to look at something. She followed him back to the front of the mill house. And, lo and behold, where those false panels had been, Sophie saw that a hidden drawer had opened and in it was a key. It must have unlatched when she turned the mill house wheel. She wondered if the key might open the house. She took it out and tried it. As the door swung inwards, Sophie drew in her breath. There were all kinds of treasures in this mill house, and Sophie was overwhelmed with the images.

Sophie discovered many things on the journey through the surrounding villages, the Land of the Contrarians, in the stillness of the waters, and in the walk through the woods. She realized that she had really been afraid of just three things.

1. She had thought that she was bad and didn't deserve love and happiness.

2. She had been afraid that if she broke the rules imposed by others that they would come after her, kick her out of town, and leave her to die.

3. She was afraid that no one was there for her, and there would be no one in her life, and she would always be alone.

But as she saw the treasures in the house, she realized that they were ones *she* had hidden a long time ago. Her caring and compassion was buried deep in her inner child's heart, and now it was time to let them out and be who she was destined to be. She had lived by the rules of others for fear that her parents would kick her out, and she would have no roof over her head, or the families she cleaned house for would fire her. Now she could live on her own terms because the magical mill house belonged to whoever found the key.

"Smart choice," Sophie she said to herself. And as she thought through all the places on her journey, she realized there had always been someone with her. Even if it wasn't a member of her immediate family, she was really never alone.

With that she wandered into the living room of her wonderful mill house. As she watched the ebb and flow of the water, she realized that the gnome was still outside. When she went to find him, she saw he had been joined by some friends. Everyone had heard how she had solved the mystery of the mill house and wanted to see who had been wise enough to figure it out. She spotted Humphrey, Glenda, and many of the creatures of the woods, even some of the Contrarians who had learned new ways were there.

She walked up to the helpful gnome and again asked him for his name.

"My dear, let me introduce myself. My name is Hugh, which means heart. While you are wise as your name implies, sometimes you just gotta have heart. That is why Humphrey thought to send me, Hugh the big-hearted gnome, to help you out."

With that she invited everyone to celebrate the solving of the mill house mystery. Sophie knew she would work with her friends, family, and others in finding how to create a lucrative training and coaching business. While she would be aware of the rules of others, she would follow the path in her heart, knowing that was good enough. And even her contrarian skills would serve her, not in finding obstacles but in solving problems that might arise. After all, she had solved the mystery of the mill house after all these years. With the image of the lotus for inspiration, the lucky key on a cord around her neck, and the picture of Humphrey, Glenda, and Hugh on her mantle, Sophie knew she had found the heart of her future.

Chapter Six
Return Again

Sophie sighed as she sat down on the new couch she had purchased for the living room of the mill house cottage. She loved the cottage with all its treasures and hidden spaces, yet it felt like something was missing. She had hoped that a new piece of furniture in some of her favorite colors would make the difference. Even with the beautiful patterns of turquoise and violet, it didn't lift her mood.

She had enjoyed her time in the cottage these last few years, exploring the area and meeting new friends. She had stayed in touch with Humphrey, Hugh, and Glenda as well. Humphrey had introduced her to LouLou Belle who shared some of her approaches to transformation along with a shiny trinket or two (or three). She had a monthly study group with a few of the Contrarians (Maria, Gina, and Sam) where they used their skills to solve problems and help each other. Yet something didn't feel right or at least not complete.

Sophie took out her journal and began to write. Maybe doing some writing will allow me to uncover what I seem unable to see, she thought. Even without a specific focus, the words started flowing. It didn't seem like they made sense or created a complete picture, but the simple act of writing helped her experience a strong sense of calm. Sophie was about to drift off when there was a loud tapping at the door. She wondered who it could be. She considered disregarding the tapping, but it continued and she hated to ignore people.

She walked over to the door, looked through the peep hole and saw one of the members of the Contrarian study group. Sophie carefully opened the door to allow Maria to come into the cottage. Maria looked anxious to share something, and Sophie invited her sit on the turquoise and violet couch. She poured her a glass of water that she captured from the water wheel on the side of the house.

As she sat down on the couch, Sophie could sense the tenseness in Maria's energy and asked her what had happened.

"You know the idea we discussed at our last study group? I thought I had all the counter-examples and contrarian ideas worked out, but then Sam came up with another reason it wouldn't work and now I'm stumped. Plus, Gina started spouting all these different approaches I should try. The number of options for accomplishing my vision and goal is endless, making it feel overwhelmingly impossible."

Sophie decided to ask Maria a few questions to see if she could release the log jam of Contrarian obstacles. She knew that Contrarians could get caught in a trap of endless naysaying, and it was important to help create a more positive perspective. Without that shift, she recognized the naysaying would turn inward, and Maria would start to bully and sabotage herself, and then nothing short of Humphrey's or LouLou Belle's magic would help.

She went over to the cabinet that contained all her pads of paper and colored pens and pencils. She suggested they sit in the dining room with its big table which would give them plenty of room to create. She suggested they start with Maria's vision.

Step by step they outlined the vision that inspired her and the resources she would need to achieve it. Those steps were fairly clear as Maria had already done this work. Next Sophie asked Maria how committed she was to getting to her vision as a way to confirm how easily Maria would be knocked off her path. It felt like Maria was pretty committed to a clear outcome and knew how to get there. This knowledge made it really confusing to Sophie as to why Maria was listening to what others had to say.

Next, she asked Maria what Sam and Gina had said.

"Well, Sam said that no one would be interested in what I have to offer. Gina said I need to have a clear message, but she didn't like any of the ones I created. Then she said I need to spend at least 20 hours a week going to different meetings to build my network. And then she said, in addition to my clear 30-second message, I need one that is only three words and another that is six words and then one that is seven words and then 17 words. I need to send out daily social media posts on at least five different platforms, and there have to be offers and calls to action included. And then, on top of that, I have to make sure that everyone who buys from me is willing to also refer someone to me and, in order to make that happen, I have to create a referral payment plan. I need to have a free giveaway that will get peoples' attention so they will want to sign up for my list, and I should expect that only one in 100 will have any interest in what it is I am trying to sell."

Maria then went on to further explain that she found it extremely confusing because she knew other people doing the same thing who didn't have to do nearly the number of things that were being suggested.

Sophie suggested that Maria stand, take a deep breath, and move one step forward and see what, if anything, shifted. Nothing did.

"Okay, let's try this a different way," Sophie said. "Let's lay out a timeline and see how it feels to walk through the steps."

Maria agreed. Sophie had Maria choose a floor marker to represent where she was starting from and another to represent her vision. She explained that visions can change over time and asked Maria if she was okay if that was the case. Maria confirmed that while she was committed to her vision, she wasn't so attached to it that she wouldn't change it.

When Maria stepped onto the floor marker for her vision, Sophie could see her energy change. A smile appeared on Maria's face; her body relaxed; it was like the vision caused her to blossom. While she stood there, Sophie asked Maria if she felt that what Sam said was true—that no one would be interested in what she had to offer? Maria felt certain that she could achieve her vision or some variation of it.

Next Sophie had her write down each of the items that Gina had told her were needed on separate pieces of paper. She then asked Maria to place each piece of paper where she felt it belonged in the space between where was now and her vision. She was building a systemic constellation to create a three-dimensional perspective, but she could sense that in doing this exercise Maria was starting to hyperventilate. Instead of continuing Sophie asked Maria to come sit with her on the couch. While it was important to be open to feedback and the opinion of others, it seemed it had undermined Maria's sense of self.

Sophie knew she could help Maria through this seeming morass to a clear outcome; however, since they were part of the same study group, she felt an ethical obligation to get assistance from other helpful resources. She went to her phone and put out the call for assistance to Humphrey. She asked him if he would bring Glenda, LouLou Belle, and Hugh with him. Any magical tools they had to help uncover possibilities, overcome obstacles, provide perspective, and nurture a dream would be of great assistance.

As they each arrived, Sophie welcomed them into her home. They gathered around the dining room table and shared what they had brought to assist Maria in stepping out of the obstacle morass and onto a clear path forward.

Humphrey went first. He was, of course, wearing his green hat and had brought along his kaleidoscope and snow globe. He shared with the group that the kaleidoscope was a way to change your perspective and view things differently. He passed the kaleidoscope around the table and everyone was able to see how it created diverse combinations of colors and changed how things looked. As they were doing that, he gave the snow globe a good shake, and everyone could see the sparkles and other objects that appeared. The magic of these items truly made it seem like the possibilities were endless.

Glenda went next. She shared about her journey to the other side of the rainbow and how she was able to bring color into her life while defining her perfect second career. She felt color was especially important to support people in shifting their emotions, uncovering the truth of who they are, and ensuring there was a balance in one's body, mind, soul, and surroundings. She let everyone know she had helped choose Sophie's new sofa. The violet and turquoise combination supported Sophie's work of bringing transformation out to the world. She also reminded the group that even to this day not everyone in the kingdom could see the colors she shared, and her focus was on those who chose to perceive them.

LouLou Belle picked up a box of smooth stones she had placed on the floor. When she heard Humphrey describe the situation on the phone, she felt that bringing them along would create a clear pathway. She shared that now along with a beautiful ceramic container with the word "gratitude" etched on the outside. There were small slips of cardboard with words like sunshine, friends, and joy written on them. There were also blank slips where you could write your own words as a way to nurture your dream. Just in case, she took out the small bottle of magic sparkles. The stones, the ceramic container with words, and the magic sparkles were all tools of transformation.

Hugh shared that he wasn't as involved with transformation and healing as everyone else. However, he had played an important role in helping Sophie find the key to her heart's desire and wanted to be supportive of Maria. He had brought along some lovely roses, yummy chocolates and pastries, and a beautiful glass heart.

They started by asking Maria if she was willing to look at possibilities and pathways to her dream rather than focus on the obstacles. She said she was. They went over to where Sophie had laid out the markers and removed all but the ones for current situation and future vision. They let her know they were going to take turns asking her a series of questions. If Maria replied "yes" in response, she would need to make an I AM statement to indicate her agreement.

The questions were as follow:

1. Are you committed to creating a prosperous business?

2. Are you clear and aligned (body, mind, and soul) to your vision?

3. Do you accept that you are an expert yet can learn more?

4. Are you open to possibilities and clues?

5. Do you acknowledge you are connected to Source?

6. Are you willing to take right and intentional action?

7. Are you able to hold yourself accountable?

8. Are you willing to trust, allow, and receive?

9. Can you see all you have to be grateful, thankful, and appreciative for?

10. Can you say with confidence, "I am an amazingly successful and valued businessperson who helps others"?

Maria answered "yes" to each question. For the ones where she sounded a bit uncertain, all five of them asked her. By the time she had responded five times, her voice was strong as she stated, "I am an amazingly successful and valued businessperson who helps others."

They sat down again at the dining room table, and Sophie went to make some tea and coffee to go with the sweets that Hugh had brought. LouLou Belle placed the smooth stones in front of Maria along with some pens of sparkly, multicolored ink. She reminded her of the pathway she created and asked her to write on the individual stones: committed, clear alignment, expert, possibilities, source, action, accountable, and grateful. She then handed Maria a larger stone and suggested she write amazingly successful and valued.

After the ink on the stones had dried and the group had finished their snacks, they went back to the space where Maria had walked the pathway to her vision. She stepped through it a second time, placing each stone as a marker on the pathway. As she did, she realized these were her inner resources, her inner team of allies who would support her in moving forward no matter what Sam, Gina, or others said.

As Maria was walking her pathway, an insight popped into Sophie's head. She saw clearly how this group created a really powerful support structure. While Sophie was grateful she had the wisdom to help solve a problem for Maria, she realized it was the group working together as a team who created the pathway.

Each had something amazing to contribute. Humphrey's journey had been about re-writing his story to find his place and sense of belonging. LouLou Belle had found possibilities through sharing her gifts. Glenda had found her purpose and passion by finding her tribe: those who wished to change. Hugh was all about being kind, sweet, and coming from the heart.

After Maria placed the stone with her vision, she looked up and smiled. She told them she had the perfect place at her home to put all the stones and would walk the pathway often. She thanked everyone for their help and support and knew she would hold them in her heart as she followed the pathway and watched her dream unfold.

Sophie then asked everyone to share one final thought before they all went on their way. Hugh had already given Maria the glass heart and said it was to remind her to be kind to herself and others. LouLou Belle presented Maria with a small bag of crystals to remind her of the value in sharing her gifts. Glenda reminded her to focus on people who supported her on her path and the ones who were interested in what she had to offer. Humphrey said he looked forward to seeing the book that Maria would write based on finding her place and sense of self on the pathway to business success.

As they all walked to the door, Sophie smiled to herself thinking she had made a very wise choice in who she had invited to help Maria move beyond her doubts and Contrarian thoughts and step onto the pathway to her vision.

After everyone had left and she closed the door, for some reason in that moment Sophie was reminded of a song she had heard at one of the coach training retreats she had attended. It was entitled "Return Again" by Shaina Noll and started with "Return again, return again. Return to the land of your soul."

Chapter Seven
The Story Beneath the Metaphor

Back in 1992, I started what has become a multi-decade healing and learning journey; it started with a physical condition (fibroids). I went to a doctor who, before even examining me, emphatically stated I had to have them surgically removed. My logical, problem-solving brain, along with my distaste for those who tell me what I "must" do, caused me to turn around and head right out the door never to return.

Pondering what was next, I remembered back to when I was introduced to Edgar Cayce and sought out a local practitioner. While working with her, she recommended other resources and the search for healing began. A small lymphatic blockage sent me to a lymphatic massage practitioner. She successfully addressed the blockage and became an amazing resource over the years as she shared new approaches to support health and healing. Through the following seven years, I was introduced to many wonderful people who practiced an array of approaches. All were instrumental on that first part of my journey.

While the symptoms from my fibroids were not severe, the fibroids themselves kept increasing in number and size resulting in a negative impact on other organs. Finally, my doctor said I needed to do something and since embolization had become an option, I chose that approach. I had investigated numerous medical procedures and it was the least invasive and had become an insurance-approved practice the prior year. Although my healing took longer than the time they indicated, the outcome was positive.

Six months after the embolization, I was outside mulching my garden and started having trouble breathing. I knew I had allergies and didn't think much of it, but it persisted and off I went to my primary care doctor. He diagnosed me with asthma and gave me instructions as to what to do. I went into extreme resistance; after all, I had been a smoker for 20 years and never had breathing problems. My resistance turned against me, and I ended up on steroids and had to stay home from work for a week.

During my week at home, I received a clear insight, a message, that there were three seven-year phases to my journey. The message provided clarity about each of the stages. The first one, which was ending, was about experiencing various healing approaches. The second was about learning approaches I could use for myself and share with others. The third one was about sharing my wisdom with the world.

Based on the message about starting a learning journey, during my next visit to the lymphatic massage practitioner, I asked her what she suggested for a good first class. She recommended Silva Mind Control, and I found two groups that held classes (one in Massachusetts and the other in Connecticut). I opted for a workshop in Connecticut, and, while it was interesting, I didn't find it compelling. Then a fascinating thing happened because of feedback from a 360 assessment at work.

I was given feedback about the intensity of my communication and my overuse of "yeah but." I happened to look at the brochure from the Massachusetts group that taught Silva and noticed that they offered NLP (Neuro-Linguistic Programming) training. One of the selling points was that it helped with communication issues, and I decided to sign up. Many deeply buried issues appeared during that 18-day training, which took place over six months. A kaleidoscope of memories, picture after picture of long-buried events, came rushing to the surface. It was painfully overwhelming, but I remained committed to the journey and chose to continue.

At some point during the NLP trainings, we were given an assignment to write a metaphorical hero's journey. We were informed about the assignment but had not yet received any instructions. Disliking the unknown and wanting to make sure I did it right, I ruminated and ruminated, trying to figure out how to get ahead of the assignment. Then one day a story started to write itself. It was a most unusual experience. While I still cannot explain how it happened, it became a story within the story of that metaphorical journey. Humphrey, the gnome dressed as an elf, was born.

The learning journey continued through NLP Practitioner, Master Practitioner, Health Practitioner, Resource Assistant, Coach, and Hypnosis in that first phase. There was energy healing with Reiki, learning about the vibration of color with Aura-Soma, and much more. The most intense portion of the training took place during the third seven-year phase.

In one of the NLP classes, I was introduced to the concept of the shadow and Debbie Ford's book, *The Dark Side of the Light Chasers*, was recommended. I read and loved it, and then in a workshop one day someone out of the blue said, "Did you know that Debbie Ford offers a coaching program?" I was both amazed at the synchronicity and intrigued at the opportunity. Despite all the work over 14 years, I continued to feel a split, almost like I was two different people, and shadow work sounded like it might help.

I called and was accepted upon condition of my attendance at The Shadow Process workshop. It was an amazing experience and was followed by coach trainings at JFK University and The Ford Institute in Best Year, Blueprint, and Spiritual Divorce Integrative Coaching.

Yet another experience led me to Voice Dialogue supporting me in working through the internal conflicts and double binds I had created as a survival strategy. A practitioner recommended Family Constellations "if

I had any issues with family." A random mention of a modality used to address a money block led me to Somatic Repatterning and a two-year effort to have the creator teach me. These are among the 14 certifications I have achieved and the 100 plus modalities I have experienced.

Through it all, I learned that while the experiences of my childhood didn't break me, they did shatter me into many different pieces. They also contained a "golden lesson" that led me to work with teams and individuals ensuring everyone's value was seen and voice was heard—even better if one could find synergy in those with opposite talents (i.e. creative and analytical).

I have heard many amazing stories of people who have overcome extreme verbal abuse, emotional abuse, sexual abuse, poverty, illness, and the list goes on. There are those who are impacted by narcissistic parents, parents who neglect their children, and those who hover too close. There are the impacts of trauma, natural disasters, patterns in our family history, secrets and hidden truths, children taking on too much responsibility—all of which create our unique life mosaic.

In my case, the combination of a physical condition, betrayal, and trauma created by other children, being underestimated because I was a female and the younger sibling of very talented older brothers, and an environment of living in constant fear with no safe place to be resulted in physical disease, interpersonal challenges, and a feeling I never belonged.

For those who say that children who are bullied should just get over it, I share the triple whammy from my thirteenth year which instilled deeply subconscious patterns.

- The first trauma was when my "so-called" best friend stood up in the cafeteria and shared my bed wetting secret. In that moment, I wanted to disappear and did my best to stay invisible for most of my life.

- The second was an incident that revealed itself in 2012 thanks to an interesting combination of factors leading to a spontaneous trauma release through NLP. A small group of girls blocked me as I walked down a school corridor and then somehow backed me into the girls' bathroom. With my back literally against the wall, a pattern of wanting to die but with an intense need to live was established. Glimpses of it surfaced in the intensity of my communication style especially when I felt "backed up against a wall." It also created a lifelong inner conflict of doing everything possible to survive while being an expert in self-sabotage.

- The third was also created by being a bed wetter sent to sleepaway camp. In year two, night after night for the weeks I was there, the other girls verbally tormented me. The repetitive nature of that experience ensured that it has stayed tightly locked up. But it was bad enough that when I came home that summer, I told my mother I was never going back, and she couldn't make me. I never did return, and the memories are still buried.

The initial story of Humphrey and some of the other chapters were written during the NLP classes I took and the work I did with an improv coach—all focused on uncovering the traumas, words, feelings, and thoughts I had buried in order to survive that were impacting my physical health, my career, and my relationships with friends and family among others.

My original intention was to publish the story with proceeds going to an organization who works to prevent bullying. Then I decided it was too short, and I would finalize it and keep it just for me. But recently this chapter came into my mind. Along with that, the continued insights from family constellations about how what we exclude or take out of place impacts us, the more I see the bullying that is happening every day, and the more I find my voice, the more I realized this book needed to be brought into the light.

My intensity drove people away and was frequently perceived as anger. The wall (or, as one person called it, scaffolding) I put up to protect myself kept me from fully sharing my gifts and was received as aloofness and sometimes arrogance. The traumas I buried deep inside led to disease and giving off confused messages to others and myself— wanting to be visible yet needing to hide, wanting to excel while trying to fail, wanting to connect while uncertain how.

Everyone's journey starts in a different place whether it be a health condition, a relationship breakup, the loss of a job or money. For some it is the illness or death of a child. Sometimes it is driven simply by a curiosity to know more or a pull to do something different with their life. Sometimes it starts in childhood and other times it appears later in life.

My hope is that, through the story of Humphrey (the storyteller I have become) and LouLou Belle (the purveyor of many gifts of transformation that I embody), that the impact of bullying is seen, that the need to fit into your family and community is felt, and that it is understood that what we present on the outside is only a small part of the truth of who we are.

Be kind to yourself. Shine your light. Live your value.

To your blossoming,
Mindy and my inner team: Humphrey, LouLouBelle, Glenda, Hugh, and Sophie

LouLou Belle's Epilogue

As mentioned, LouLou Belle had the gift of transformational tools. As all good transformational practitioners are aware, it is important to do your own work in order to be as clean of your agenda as possible in supporting your clients. In doing so, LouLou Belle looked at the NLP Identity Matrix which has a series of questions connected to who you do and don't want to be. Here is the result of her work. I especially like the part about the soil tiller.

LouLou Belle took a journey through the forest towards the highest mountain peak in order to observe a magnificent shining star that had been noted for its colorful reflection. As she got closer to the mountain, she grew tired and decided to take a nap. She was unaware that if she delayed too long she would miss seeing what was the most powerful force of the universe. During her nap, a witch came upon her and threw a powdery substance in the air, which fell on her and kept her sleeping and sleeping for what seemed like hours. LouLou Belle somehow realized that she had been drugged and became angry since all she had done was go on an adventure. In her mind's eye, she was able to conjure up a soil tiller and, as it turned over the earth, the hold of the powder dissipated, and the witch was buried underneath the fresh dirt.

She woke up from her nap with a confident strength that propelled her towards the mountain. Step by step, one foot in front of the other, she moved forward on her journey. As she climbed the mountain, she was reminded of the Glastonbury Tor and, even though she felt unstable and uncertain, knew that what she was climbing towards was magnificent and holy. She found a comfortable spot in a sheltered area and gazed up at the sky. While the color of the sky was becoming darker, a magnificent shining star appeared that illuminated everything for miles around. The power of the light was intense and allowed even stagnant ponds to flow freely. She had arrived in time to capture this perfect and powerful moment and bring within herself the powerful light that shifts stagnation to flow.

Epilogue

My path inward began initially because of a physical symptom, and I followed that path with the assistance of many wonderful people. It later expanded to explore the identified interpersonal challenges and continued to unfold. The initial 21-year journey that started because of a visit to the doctor has ended, and a new journey began upon my leaving the corporate world.

I now understand that I disconnected from my body because I felt it had betrayed me. I created separation from my family because I thought I didn't belong. I buried my soul under more layers than I can count. I touched the edges of my purpose but surrounded it with doubts and comparison. My true journey back was not just through my physical body but the emotions, beliefs, interpretations, strategies, and experiences that make up my life mosaic.

The connection between them was highlighted for me in an experience I had a few years ago.

I decided to do a live cell analysis where they take a drop of blood, place it on a microscope, and interpret what it says about your digestion and other bodily functions. Somehow on this one particular day, we got around to discussing emotions. Before we started the conversation, the blood sample had been taken and was on the slide under the microscope where we could both see it. During the exchange, the word terror came up. (Several people have described certain events as my being terrorized.) When that word came out of my mouth, those blood cells sitting on the slide literally fled to the outside edges of the slide. The look of surprise and amazement on the practitioner's face made the impact even more powerful.

Think the mean and nasty things you say and do to others and to yourself don't have a lasting impact? Think again.

Be kind to yourself and allow the truth of who you are to blossom and grow and have a positive impact on the world.

Acknowledgments

Given the duration of my healing, learning, and writing journey, there are many individuals to acknowledge.

Thank you to the many amazing practitioners who have helped my physical body to heal. From bodyworkers to acupuncturists, kinesiologists, and more—too numerous to name.

The late Connie McGrath, who helped heal my body, started me on my learning journey and allowed me to share my gifts with her before she passed. Her influence on me is immeasurable. I loved the sparkles and sunshine she shared.

Marilou Seavey, extraordinary teacher of NLP who in addition to teaching me helped me process the overwhelming number of memories that appeared after the first class. I will never forget the space you held during the viscerally impactful trauma release that helped explain so much.

The late Debbie Ford and all those at The Ford Institute. The amazing power of the work helped the source of "my split" come to the surface. The magic and power of Integrative Coaching continues to be evident with every client I take through it.

Ilene Myers and Jaye Lasko, my amazing Somatic Repatterning practitioners/teachers. It was well worth the two-year effort to learn this life-changing work. Thank you to Cheryl Ferrari for the initial introduction.

While I had no plans to take Voice Dialogue training, J. Tamar Stone, my sessions with you convinced me otherwise. Thank you for helping me find a path to wholeness including a better understanding of how shopping and disconnected go together.

I discovered Aura-Soma accidentally when a book caught my attention at a Whole Foods store. The journey to understand this amazing color system, the learning, the associated travel, and the friends, have changed my life forever. Color really does have a language.

Peter and Jamy Faust who first introduced me to Family Constellations in 2004 and who along with Judy Wilkins-Smith have helped me understand and now share the power of healing the systemic patterns in our ancestry while transforming my own family patterns in the process.

The other wonderful practitioners who have been with me at different times throughout this journey including Toni Stevens (Bodytalk), Anne Drake (Shamanism), and Daena Giardella (Improvisational Coaching), and JoAnn Gorka (Healing Touch).

Katrina Pfannkuch, your editing support over the last four years has been invaluable in helping me build my writing skill and more fully step into my love of writing.

Drew Becker and Diana Henderson for your help in formatting and editing this book. Thank you for your support and guidance in getting my first solo book into print.

Nicole Jeska for bringing the characters in this book to life through your illustrations.

My clients. While many choose to remain anonymous, the transformations you experience inspire me every day and remind me of the importance of sharing this transformational work.

To my brothers. When I said I was the younger sister of three very talented older brothers, it was the truth. Glad I found my way back to you.

My sister-in-law Marlene for introducing me to the work of Edgar Cayce, which ultimately was the start of my healing journey.

My friends, those who have seen through to the truth of who I am. You are part of the reason I was able to live this journey.

The bullies and other naysayers. While you may not remember who you are, I do. While you had no right, I better understand why. As they say, what doesn't kill you makes you stronger. Sometimes you have to experience something so that you learn to do the opposite.

About the Author

Mindy Schrager is an ICF ACC credentialed coach and systemic facilitator whose passion for transformational work grew out of her career success in building strong, well balanced teams, combined with a very powerful personal discovery journey.

Her facilitation and leadership approach focuses on empowering team members to work more effectively together. By understanding and valuing the similarities and differences among them, Mindy's teams throughout her thirty-four years of corporate experience created more cohesive, desired results that also enabled everyone to focus on individual strengths—and balance out weaknesses.

The more Mindy practiced transformational perspectives, she began to clearly see how business team alignment and synergy is as important as the alignment of all the parts of our "inner team". In both worlds, we work towards more collaborative connections, expansive results, clear alignment between our values and outcomes, and a healthy sense of self-awareness. The result? We learn to release old ways of being and create new pathways for effective, healthy life strategies.

Mindy Schrager is a first time solo author, a long-time blogger and is dedicated to transformational work for individuals and teams providing insights, perspectives and practical tools that create harmony within teams and ourselves.

If you decide to look for transformational resources as you traverse your own personal journey, please contact me through my website at *www.systemsofchange.com*

BONUS

Each chapter of the book ties to a specific transformational concept. Take a brief "quiz" associated with each concept to gain a better understanding of where you are on your own transformational journey Check out the chapter summary that most resonates for you and take that quiz or look at all five. Each has a transformational process you can use to create new pathways and possibilities. To access this information go to: *https://systemsofchange.com/bonus/*

9/7

CPSIA information can be obtained
at www.ICGtesting.com
Printed in the USA
BVHW090401071120
592655BV00001B/2